EMPOWERMENT

A Practical Guide for Success

Cynthia D. Scott, Ph.D., M.P.H.
Dennis T. Jaffe, Ph.D.

A FIFTY-MINUTE™ SERIES BOOK

CRISP PUBLICATIONS, INC.
Menlo Park, California

DISTRIBUTED BY
FLEX TRAINING LTD
9-15 Hitchin Street
Baldock
Herts. SG7 6AL
Tel: 01462 895544
Fax: 01462 892417

EMPOWERMENT

A Practical Guide for Success

Cynthia D. Scott, Ph.D., M.P.H.
Dennis T. Jaffe, Ph.D.

CREDITS
Editor: **Tony Hicks**
Layout and Composition: **Interface Studio**
Cover Design: **Carol Harris**
Artwork: **Ralph Mapson**

Copyright © 1991 by Crisp Publications, Inc.
Printed in the United States of America

English language Crisp books are distributed worldwide. Our major international distributors include:

CANADA: Reid Publishing Ltd., Box 69559—109 Thomas St., Oakville, Ontario, Canada L6J 7R4. TEL: (905) 842-4428, FAX: (905) 842-9327

Raincoast Books Distribution Ltd., 112 East 3rd Avenue, Vancouver, British Columbia, Canada V5T 1C8. TEL: (604) 873-6581, FAX: (604) 874-2711

AUSTRALIA: Career Builders, P.O. Box 1051, Springwood, Brisbane, Queensland, Australia 4127. TEL: 841-1061, FAX: 841-1580

NEW ZEALAND: Career Builders, P.O. Box 571, Manurewa, Auckland, New Zealand. TEL: 266-5276, FAX: 266-4152

JAPAN: Phoenix Associates Co., Mizuho Bldg. 2-12-2, Kami Osaki, Shinagawa-Ku, Tokyo 141, Japan. TEL: 3-443-7231, FAX: 3-443-7640

Selected Crisp titles are also available in other languages. Contact International Rights Manager Suzanne Kelly at (415) 323-6100 for more information.

Library of Congress Catalog Card Number 90-84923
Scott, Cynthia D. and Jaffe, Dennis T.
Empowerment
ISBN 1-56052-096-5

This book is printed on recyclable paper with soy ink.

INTRODUCTION

This book is about the process of creating an empowered organization—increasing competitiveness and profitability by enhancing the value of the contribution of the people in your organization, work group, or team.

Empowerment is the new buzzword, taken to be the fix-all in the workplace. As every organization goes about meeting challenges and making continual work improvements, they seek the support, involvement, and commitment of their employees—what we call the ''wanna factor.'' Yet many employees appear to resist and withdraw from these well-intentioned and necessary efforts. This book is for managers to understand and lead people to build an empowered workplace. It demands creating a new type of working environment.

No Quick Fix

It takes more than a few meetings or a crash program to develop employee involvement and empowerment. It involves both managers and employees rethinking old ways and learning new ones. Whatever name is given to it, the way to achieve greater human involvement in making an organization work sometimes demands a vast shift in the way that you, as a manager, operate. In our experience with both large and small organizations, we find that the manager is a key element in creating this new workplace, sometimes even the initiator and champion of the change.

For the 1990s the major sources of competitive advantage will lie not in new technology but in the dedication, the quality of the commitment, and the competency of your work force. The results of employee energy and creativity—human capital—is the company's most important resource. Empowerment is the new fuel for the growing workplace.

The process of building a highly committed, highly effective workplace has been given many labels: participative management, quality of work life, internal service environment, alternate work arrangements, open systems planning, sociotechnical systems, work redesign, or self-management.

(continued next page)

INTRODUCTION (Continued)

Whatever you call them, empowered work relationships share power, responsibility, communication, expectations, and rewards in ways that are very different from relationships in the traditional hierarchial organization. The current environment of competition and scarce resources in business requires managers to behave differently in order to be effective and help their organizations thrive.

This book will help you think about the three elements that make up the empowered workplace:

- Mindsets
- Relationships
- Structures

Each of these dimensions of the organization must shift to create an empowered workplace, or the effort will likely be doomed in failure.

Cynthia D. Scott

Dennis T. Jaffe

Without a global revolution in the sphere of human consciousness, nothing will change for the better in the sphere of our being as humans, and the catastrophe toward which this world is headed—be it ecological, social, demographic or a general breakdown of civilization—will be unavoidable.

If we are no longer threatened by world war or by the danger that the absurd mountains of accumulated nuclear weapons might blow up the world, this does not mean that we have definitely won. We are still incapable of understanding that the only genuine backbone of all our actions, if they are to be moral, is responsibility.

Responsibility to something higher than my family, my country, my company, my success—responsibility to the order of being where all our actions are indelibly recorded and where and only where they will be properly judged.

—Vaclav Havel,
addressing a joint session of Congress, 1990

CONTENTS

INTRODUCTION i

CHAPTER 1 The Road to Empowerment 1

CHAPTER 2 From the Pyramid to the Circle 11

CHAPTER 3 Testing the Climate for Empowerment 21

CHAPTER 4 Three Paths to Empowerment 27

CHAPTER 5 Motivating Through Self-Esteem 39

CHAPTER 6 Developing Collaborative Relationships 51

CHAPTER 7 Establishing Facilitative Leadership 61

CHAPTER 8 Building Empowered Teams 69

CHAPTER 9 Influencing Organizational Change 85

CHAPTER

1

The Road to Empowerment

THE ROAD TO EMPOWERMENT

The foundation of national wealth is really people—the human capital represented by their knowledge, skills, organizations, and motivations. The primary assets of a modern corporation leave the workplace each night to go home to dinner.

—Hudson Institute, *Workforce 2000*

EMPOWERMENT TIP

As a manager, you have to give up power and control over your people, to gain higher effectiveness, motivation, and productivity. Empowerment is an entirely different way of people working together.

Why Empowerment?

The organization is under attack from outside and from within. Externally, heightened global competition, incredibly fast changes, new demands for quality and service, and limited resources demand quick responses from the organization. Internally, employees are feeling betrayed, let down, and burned out, as they feel frustrated by an organization that is making new demands on them and changing the rules of the game. At the same time, they are also demanding more meaning, more candor, and more fulfillment from their work.

The organization must adapt and grow and learn new ways to get the job done. Employees are uncertain of their commitment or responsibility.

Caught in the middle is the manager, who feels pressed by new demands from outside and from above and must get a team on board to make the organization work.

What is Empowerment?

People want to make a difference, and the organization desperately needs them to. Yet frustration results because employees, managers, and organizations don't know how to take advantage of the human creativity and initiative that is there for the asking. The traditional organization needed only the bodies of employees doing their clearly defined jobs and not asking questions. Today's workplace needs employees who can make decisions, who can invent solutions to problems, who can take initiative, and who are accountable for results.

What is empowerment? **Empowerment is a fundamentally different way of working together.**

- **Employees** feel responsible not just for doing a job, but also for making the whole organization work better. The new employee is an active problem solver who helps plan how to get things done and then does them.

- **Teams** work together to improve their performance continually, achieving higher levels of productivity.

- **Organizations** are structured in such a way that people feel that they are able to achieve the results they want, that they can do what needs to be done, not just what is required of them and be rewarded for doing so.

The empowered workplace is characterized by:

- Enhancing the content of the work
- Expanding the skills and tasks that make up a job
- Liberating creativity and innovation
- Greater control over decisions about work
- Completing a whole task rather than just portions of it
- Customer satisfaction
- Marketplace orientation

The empowered workplace stems from a new relationship between employees and a new relationship between people and the organization. They are partners. Everyone not only feels responsible for their jobs, but feels some sense of ownership of the whole. The work team is not just a reactor to demands, it is also an initiator of action. The employee is a decision maker, not a follower. Everyone feels that they are continually learning and developing new skills to meet new demands.

From the Inside—To the Outside

Empowerment is often thought to be something you do to other people.

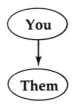

In fact, it is more of a **process**, something that happens in a relationship between people.

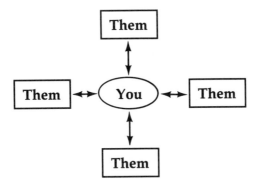

Empowerment is not a set of techniques, but rather a way of constructing an inner understanding of the relationship between yourself and the people you work with.

One way of understanding this is to notice the difference in attitude between a person who says "I do what I am" and a person who says "I am what I do." The person who says "I am a production manager" derives identity from external cues such as job title, or company. The person who says "I manage production" finds identity from cherished attitudes, beliefs, and values.

This may seem like a minimal shift, but it tends to make a big difference in understanding empowerment.

What do you say when someone asks you, "What do you do?" Write your answer here:

From the Outside—To the Inside (Continued)

Empowerment begins with a shift within the manager—understanding that to empower is not to lose control but to gain control.

Empowerment must take root in the behavior and the mind set of the whole organization, the manager, and the employees. It is a fundamentally different orientation toward working together.

For example, in a traditional hierarchy, you look toward one person—the boss—for direction and authority. In an empowered, collaborative workplace, you look toward everyone, and listen to yourself as well, before acting.

Empowerment is good news for managers, although it takes adjustment before you can experience the benefits. Instead of having sole responsibility, the manager has help. Instead of feeling ''I'' have to get it done, the manager can say ''we'' have to do it together.

An empowered workplace is one where teams of people work together, collaborating on getting the job done. This is quite different from the traditional competitive workplace, where each individual employee was engaged in a race with the others to get things done. In an empowered workplace, people can count on each other, rather than just work on their own.

Think of the most empowered workplace you have known. What were some of the things that made it that way? List them here:

_____

_____

_____

_____

_____

Freedom versus Control

Traditionally, the role of the manager was to keep processes and people under tight control. The best manager kept the tightest reins on people. Employees' behavior had to be watched and controlled by supervisors and managers.

The new workplace is one where people are empowered to make their own decisions and manage themselves. Empowerment is quite different from the traditional notion of control. It is an environment where people want to be responsible and are free to take action. But too much personal freedom would lead to chaos.

You, as a manager or supervisor, probably feel that you are caught between imposing control and allowing personal freedom. You may feel that control and freedom are opposite ends of a spectrum—that you have to choose one or the other. But looking again, you may see that in any organization some things need to be tightly controlled, while other areas of work can be left to individual freedom and initiative.

You want to keep tight control over quality and resources. But you want to enhance individual creativity, make people responsible for results, and invite them to develop high commitment to their work. Empowerment is finding the right balance.

Think of your organization.

What processes need to be tightly controlled? List them here:

_____

_____

_____

What processes need to be left to personal initiative? List them here:

_____

_____

_____

The Empowerment Balance

Think of freedom and control in relationship to each other. An organization can be high in both, or in either one. In an empowered workplace, paradoxically, people feel *both* personal freedom and control (or coordination). On the graphs below, plot yourself, your team, and organization.

Yourself

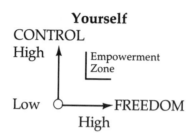

Your Team

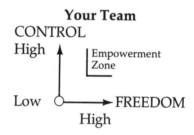

Your Organization

You might ask your other team members to discuss this issue. An effective organization has a balance of control and freedom. Like this:

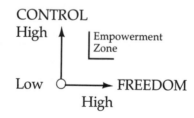

Checking Your Empowerment Level

Here are some signs of an unempowered workplace. How many do you find in your workplace? Put a check mark ☑ next to them.

- ☐ People aren't very excited about their work.
- ☐ People feel very negative.
- ☐ People only do what they are supposed to do.
- ☐ Nobody says what is on their mind.
- ☐ People are suspicious.
- ☐ People aren't willing to help out.

Unempowered employees have the following feelings. Check those that apply to your workplace.

- ☐ They don't matter.
- ☐ They should keep their ideas to themselves.
- ☐ They "rent" their job.
- ☐ Not much of their skills and energy are needed.

Empowered employees have the following feelings. Check those that apply to your workplace.

- ☐ They feel they make a difference.
- ☐ They are responsible for their results.
- ☐ They are part of the team.
- ☐ They can use their full talents and abilities.
- ☐ They have control over how they do their jobs.
- ☐ They take initiative.

C H A P T E R

2

From the Pyramid
to the Circle

FROM THE PYRAMID TO THE CIRCLE

About 2,000 years ago, the Chinese invented hierarchy. Since then, in our military, public service, and commercial organizations alike, we've been polishing that idea. But the new-look organizations, from Apple Computer to Federal Express to Wal-Mart to Chaparral Steel, are, even as they attain monster size, fundamentally different, featuring virtually nonhierarchical ways of doing business.

—Tom Peters, *Twenty Propositions About Service*

EMPOWERMENT TIP

Every organization is evolving from the pyramid to the circle style of operating. Most changes will take you and your workplace one step in that direction.

The Evolving Organization

Since the early 1970s organizations all over the world have begun to replace the traditional highly controlled, scarcely involved structure with a new organizational environment characterized by high commitment, high involvement, and self-management. One way to look at the shift toward empowerment is to think of two basic ways to structure the organization.

The traditional organization is the pyramid, while the new, empowered organization can be thought of as looking more like a circle, or a network.

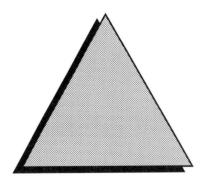

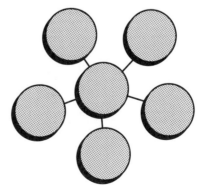

THE PYRAMID

The bureaucratic revolution of the turn of the century began a tradition of job specialization in the name of scientific management. This led to pyramidal organizations with highly specialized functions, clear boundaries, limited job descriptions, and tight control by supervisors to make sure work got done consistently and quickly. In the hierarchical, control-focused organization, the people at the very top plan and think, while the lower levels do the work.

Characteristics of the Pyramid

- Decisions are made at the top.

- Each person is clearly responsible only for their job.

- Change is slow and rare and comes only from the top.

- Feedback and communication is from the top down.

- Movement and communication between divisions is minimal.

- If you do your job you can expect job security and promotions as the organization expands.

- People focus attention upward, and the person above you is responsible for your results.

- Managers say how things are done, and what is expected.

- Employees are not expected to be highly motivated, so it is necessary to keep tight control over their behavior.

Until recently, most organizations operated roughly according to those principles.

List below some of the ways that you think the pyramid style has limitations:

_____

_____

_____

What are some of the ways that changes in your company or work team have moved away from the pyramid model?

_____

_____

_____

THE CIRCLE

The new organization form is called the circle or network, because it can be thought of as a series of coordinating groups or teams, linked by a center rather than an apex.

Characteristics of the Circle

- The customer is in the center.
- People work cooperatively together to do what is needed.
- Responsibility, skills, authority, and control are shared.
- Control and coordination come through continual communication and many decisions.
- Change is sometimes very quick, as new challenges come up.
- The key skill for an employee, and a manager, is the ability to work with others.
- There are relatively few levels of organization.
- Power comes from the ability to influence and inspire others, not from your position.
- Individuals are expected to manage themselves and are accountable to the whole; the focus is on the customer.
- Managers are the energizers, the connectors, and the empowerer of their teams.

Thinking of the circle or network, what aspects of your own organization operate like this? List them here:

_____

_____

What kinds of activity do you think the circle model accomplishes more effectively than the pyramid model? List some here:

_____

_____

What do you think are the limits and drawbacks of the circle model? List some:

_____

_____

As your organization tries to change toward the circle model, what are the obstacles that it faces along the way? List the key obstacles:

_____

_____

Where Are You?

Most organizations are somewhere between the pyramid and the circle. On the scale below, indicate where you see your team and your organization.

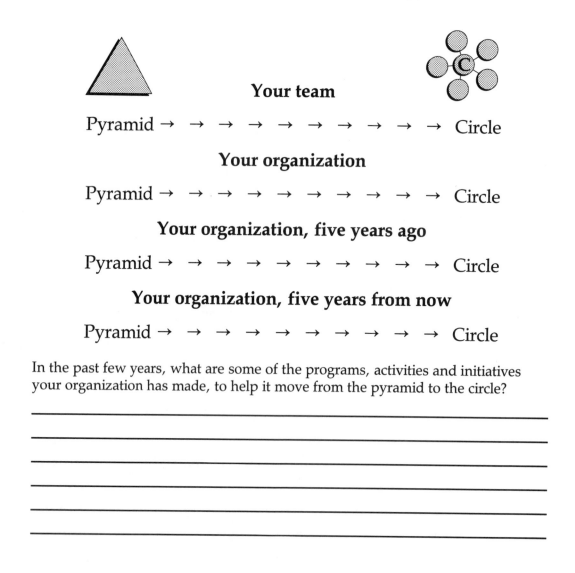

Your team

Pyramid → → → → → → → → → → Circle

Your organization

Pyramid → → → → → → → → → → Circle

Your organization, five years ago

Pyramid → → → → → → → → → → Circle

Your organization, five years from now

Pyramid → → → → → → → → → → Circle

In the past few years, what are some of the programs, activities and initiatives your organization has made, to help it move from the pyramid to the circle?

_____

_____

_____

_____

_____

Your Changing Organization

Your organization is facing new competitors, new demands, and new pressures. Change is coming more quickly. Knowing where you have been and where you are going puts you on the path to empowerment.

Think of your organization five years ago, and write down your answers to these questions:

What did an employee expect from the organization?

_____

_____

_____

What made a good job?

_____

_____

_____

What did it take to succeed in your organization?

_____

_____

_____

What were the major motivators for employees?

_____

_____

_____

How has teamwork changed?

_____

_____

_____

18

Your Changing Organization (Continued)

Imagine what your organization will be like five years from now. How will your answers change?

What will an employee expect from the organization?

_____
_____
_____

What will define a good job?

_____
_____
_____

What will it take to succeed in your organization?

_____
_____
_____

What will be the major motivators from employees?

_____
_____
_____

How will the teamwork have changed?

_____
_____
_____

Use this diagram to summarize some of the major changes that have affected your organization and that will affect your organization in the future.

FIVE YEARS AGO	NOW	FIVE YEARS AHEAD
_____	_____	_____
_____	_____	_____
_____	_____	_____
_____	_____	_____

The Road to Empowerment

The shift from the pyramid to the circle is not an easy cycle of development. In fact, being part of an organization moving from one form to the other feels pretty crazy. Change happens everywhere, and it is hard to see the reason for much of it. People feel like they are always reacting, putting out fires, don't have the time or energy to innovate or initiate.

Think of this as a journey with bridges to cross.

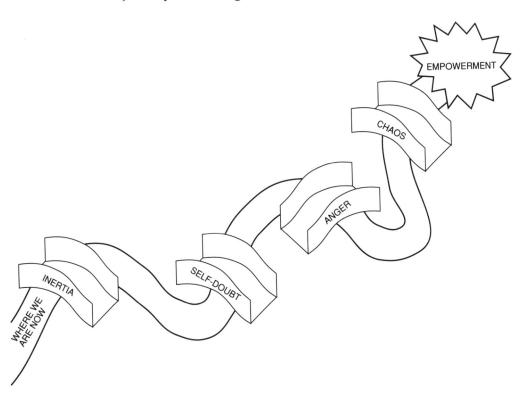

BUMPS ALONG THE WAY

There will be predictable bumps along the way. Don't get stuck. Know these bumps are there, and get encouragement and ideas when you come to them.

- **Inertia**—difficulty in deciding to get started (often seems easier to stay where you are)

- **Self Doubt**—not believing you really can create an empowered workplace

- **Anger**—blaming others for having to go through all this

- **Chaos**—Seeing so many ways to get there that you become lost along the way

C H A P T E R

3

Testing the Climate for Empowerment

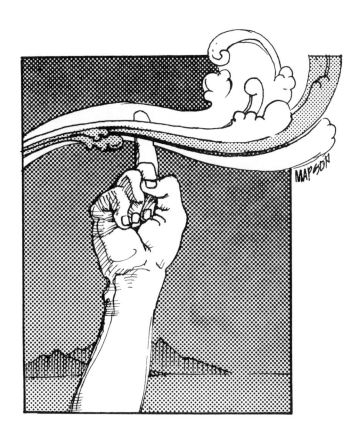

TESTING THE CLIMATE FOR EMPOWERMENT

A combination of forces—from the rapidly changing business environment to the new work force to astonishing advances in technology—is forging a breakdown of the large, traditional, hierarchical organizations that have dominated the past. We think that this dismantling will result in highly decentralized organizations in which the work of the corporation will be done in small, autonomous units linked...by new telecommunications and computer technologies. This change can turn us all into entrepreneurs and in the process will transform the role of middle management.

—Terrence Deal and Allan Kennedy, *Corporate Cultures*

EMPOWERMENT TIP

Empowerment is a quality that is reflected in every aspect of the work environment. Start by checking your level of empowerment, using an assessment tool.

Key Qualities of Empowered Workplaces

As a manager, how can you know how empowered your workplace is? Empowerment is a concept represented by many elements—personal, team, and organization—and there is not yet an agreed-upon way to measure it precisely. If you ask several workers to describe empowerment, they'll probably come up with several descriptions.

In working with organizations to improve the climate of empowerment, the following seem to be listed over and over.

- Clarity of purpose
- Morale
- Fairness
- Recognition
- Team work
- Participation
- Communication
- Healthy environment

Assessing Empowerment

The survey that follows looks at each of these areas of the organizational environment that lead to a climate of empowerment. Look to assess the level of empowerment in your company and work together.

Please fill out the survey yourself, then have your other team members fill it out.

Answer each of the questions. Consider to what degree you feel each assessment is true for your own work group.

If you feel that a statement is *very true*, circle the number 1.
If you feel that a statement is *somewhat true*, circle the number 2.
If you feel that a statement is *somewhat untrue*, circle the number 3.
If you feel that a statement is *very untrue*, circle the number 4.

EMPOWERMENT ASSESSMENT

Group

1. Clarity of Purpose

People know where they stand.	1 2 3 4
I know what is expected of me.	1 2 3 4
Tasks and responsibilities are clearly organized.	1 2 3 4
Systems and procedures are adequate.	1 2 3 4
I know what the company (team) stands for.	1 2 3 4

2. Morale

People are trusted.	1 2 3 4
Policies are flexible enough to consider personal needs.	1 2 3 4
I feel respected as a person.	1 2 3 4
Individual differences in lifestyle and values are respected.	1 2 3 4
I like working here.	1 2 3 4
There is a positive spirit.	1 2 3 4
If I had a personal problem, the company (team) would stand by me while I worked it out.	1 2 3 4

3. Fairness

I approve of the things that go on here.	1 2 3 4
People are treated fairly.	1 2 3 4
I trust what the company (team) says.	1 2 3 4

	Group
4. Recognition	
Individual effort is rewarded appropriately.	1 2 3 4
If people do something well, it is noticed.	1 2 3 4
The company (team) looks at what you can do, not who you know.	1 2 3 4
The company (team) expects the best from people.	1 2 3 4
5. Teamwork	
People help each other out.	1 2 3 4
People work together to solve difficult problems.	1 2 3 4
People care for each other.	1 2 3 4
People here are out for the company (group), not themselves.	1 2 3 4
6. Participation	
People have a voice in decisions.	1 2 3 4
Problems are shared.	1 2 3 4
People get the resources they need to do their jobs.	1 2 3 4
7. Communication	
I am kept informed of what's going on in the company.	1 2 3 4
Communication is clear and timely between groups.	1 2 3 4
I understand why things are asked of me.	1 2 3 4
8. Healthy Environment	
People are able to manage the pressure of their work.	1 2 3 4
I am not expected to do too many things.	1 2 3 4
Change is managed well.	1 2 3 4
Red tape and procedures don't interfere with getting things done.	1 2 3 4
I am able to grow and learn.	1 2 3 4
There are opportunities for career development.	1 2 3 4

To interpret your scores, turn the page.

Assessing Empowerment (Continued)

UNDERSTANDING YOUR SCORES

There are as yet no standard scores indicating what is high and low empowerment. For each of the eight areas, average the scores by dividing your total of all the numbers you circled by the number of questions in that section. If several people in a work team take this assessment, you can also average all their responses together for a group score.

Write your average scores here for each section:

1. _____
2. _____
3. _____
4. _____
5. _____
6. _____
7. _____
8. _____

Mark your two highest scores with an asterisk (*). Circle your two lowest scores.

Generally, the sections in which the average is above 2.0 raise issues you should talk about in your team.

Which areas show a lot of difference in scores between team members? Talk about it in a group.

What can you do to make changes that will lead to a more empowered workplace?

_____

_____

_____

_____

_____

C H A P T E R

4

Three Paths to Empowerment

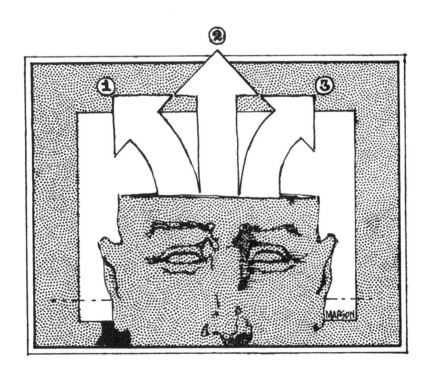

THREE PATHS TO EMPOWERMENT

There are two types of change: one that occurs within a given system which itself remains unchanged, and one whose occurrence changes the system itself. To exemplify this distinction in more behavioral terms: a person having a nightmare can do many things in his dream—run, hide, fight, scream, jump off a cliff, etc.—but no change from any one of these behaviors to another would ever terminate the nightmare. We shall henceforth refer to this kind of change as first-order change. The one way out of a dream involves a change from dreaming to waking. Waking, obviously, is no longer a part of the dream, but a change to an altogether different state. This kind of change [is] second-order change.

—Watzlawick, Weakland, and Fisch, *Change*

EMPOWERMENT TIP

Empowerment is not a single change, but a total shift of everything about the way you do business and work together. There are no short cuts.

Empowerment Is Total

Empowerment is more than a state of mind, a set of team behaviors, or organizational policies. It cannot exist unless individual attitudes and mindsets, team behaviors, and organizational values all support it. Many attempts to create organizational empowerment fail because they only create change at one of these levels.

For example, a company tries to create empowerment by running all its people through a series of off-site retreats. The experience is powerful, and the participants see all sorts of exciting possibilities. But when they return to their teams, full of energy, they feel they hit a wall. Things don't change!

First- and Second-Order Change

First- and second-order changes are very different. It is a difference not just of degree, but of quality.

Here are some examples:

SITUATION	FIRST-ORDER CHANGE	SECOND-ORDER CHANGE
Driving a car	Use gas pedal	Shift gears
Watching TV	Change channel	Turn it off
Government	Change from one dictator to another	Change from dictatorship to democracy
Meeting	Shift agenda	Use meeting facilitator
Assessing results	Increase target numbers	Focus on quality of products
Team	New procedures	New way of making decisions
Business	Reshuffle jobs	Go from pyramid to circle

In the spaces below, list some examples you can identify of first- and second-order change.

SITUATION	FIRST-ORDER CHANGE	SECOND-ORDER CHANGE
_____	_____	_____
_____	_____	_____
_____	_____	_____
_____	_____	_____
_____	_____	_____
_____	_____	_____

Moving Mindsets

The move toward empowerment, from a pyramid to a circle organization, involves a series of shifts of mind. Some of these shifts involve a drastic reorientation of the way we see our work.

For example, some of the shifts are:

From ⟶	To
powerless	empowered
waiting for orders	taking action
doing things right	doing the right thing
reactive	creative and proactive
content	process and content
quantity	quality and quantity
boss responsible	all responsible
blame placing	problem solving

What is one shift that you have noticed in your workplace?

_____

_____

What are some examples of this shift?

_____

_____

_____

_____

_____

Process, Responsibility, Learning

Empowerment involves three major shifts in mindset for everyone in an organization.

TOWARD PROCESS

In addition to reaching its goal, a work group must look at how it gets there. It must be able to reach the goal again and to do things better next time. It must develop self-awareness of how it does things, and these understandings must be shared.

TOWARD RESPONSIBILITY

In the empowered work team, everyone has the responsibility that was traditionally given the leader. If anyone sees a problem or has an idea, they are responsible for bringing it to the group. The idea must be respected, and everyone should be engaged in looking for ways to grow and develop. It's not enough for just the leadership to do this.

TOWARD LEARNING

The traditional organization was reactive, either to top management plans or to the environment. In the empowered organization, people are willing to take action, to seek out and solve problems, to take risks, to speak out, and to work together. They don't wait to be told, and they aren't paralyzed by fear or caution.

The Core Mind Shifts

The shift from getting the job done to attending to process, taking responsibility for the development of the whole organization, and solving problems using active learning, is at the core of the shift to empowerment.

Attend to Process

Take Responsibility

Seek Learning

Think of your team, and write down your answers to these questions. What processes are key to getting your job done?

_____

_____

_____

Where do the greatest problems arise?

_____

_____

_____

What major areas are you responsible for?

_____

_____

_____

What current situation could use a creative approach?

_____

_____

_____

Organizational Redesign

Workplaces today are searching for quality, for continuous improvement, for doing more with less. The empowered work team recognizes that the needed changes won't come in the form of an edict from top management.

Amid that chaos, a manager or a work team needs to initiate its own response to the changes around them. The work group can form a protective boundary, working together to respond to changes, and buffering each other from some of the stress. This is done when the work group adopts its own process of empowerment.

The team must work together. Its goals are twofold. First, operational needs must be fulfilled. The second task is to find the time to step back and look at how they are reaching their goals. They need to find the perspective to rethink each of their basic processes and redesign their ways of working. This is not a one-time event, but a continuous process. However, sometimes the redesign process must be fairly encompassing.

THE ROLE OF QUALITY

Many companies have quality-improvement programs. A quality program aims at having people look at each of their work processes, discovering sources of difficulty, defects, inefficiency, redundancy, variation, or confusion, and creating new ways to do things better. A great discovery of the quality program is often that the people who are doing a task are the best people to redesign it—not a team of outside engineers or consultants.

A work group has to take time to rethink how it does everything. Paradoxically, this is the way that a group can help move from the pyramid to the circle form of organization. Quality, participation, and continuous work improvement programs involve creating circle structures, often alongside the more traditional pyramid reporting relationships.

Levels of Change

To create real change, each of these levels of organization must experience second-order change.

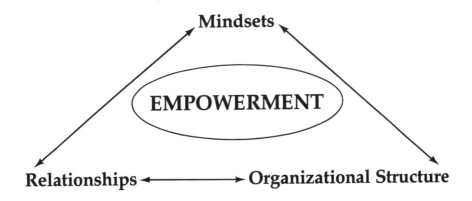

- **Mindsets** Employees take on a self-managing, accountable, responsible approach to their work.
- **Relationships** Team relationships become vital, and they focus on process as well as content. They involve communication—giving and receiving feedback.
- **Organization Structure** Policies, practices, and incentives are adopted that match the value of empowerment.

HOW TO START SECOND-ORDER CHANGE

To effect change, you must make shifts at each of these levels. Change can start at any point, but all three areas must be addressed to create a lasting impact. For example, you might begin with a training program for individuals, building awareness in new values and in change technology.

Next, you might follow it up with team sessions, creating agreements about productivity and accountability.

Next, the organization policies and structures need to support these ways with policies and other forms of top management commitment.

Write below what you could do to effect change in each level of the organization:

Mindsets _____ _____ _____

Relationships _____ _____ _____

Structures _____ _____ _____

Steps to Second-Order Change

Below is a flow chart to second-order change. Fill in steps 3 and 4, which you intend to initiate.

	Step 1 →	Step 2 →	Step 3 →	Step 4
Activity:	Briefing on empowerment	Discussion about responsibility		
Who is involved:	Team	Team		
First- or Second-order change:	First	Second		

EMPOWERMENT IS SECOND-ORDER CHANGE

The shift from the pyramid to the circle, and from traditional management to empowerment, is not a first-order change. The whole way of doing business has to change. Many managers mistakenly see empowerment as a first-order change, a simple set of new instructions. But in fact, empowerment represents a change in everything about a group, from the way that people see the organization to how they work together.

Changes To Create Empowerment

The process of empowerment works on three levels. The following are some indicators of changes that individuals, relationships, and organizational structures have made on their path to empowerment.

☑ Check the ones that you have made.

1. **Mindsets**
   - **Manager**
     - ☐ Helps employees get the job done
     - ☐ Initiates inquiry about common ways of thinking
     - ☐ Challenges assumptions
     - ☐ Encourages risk and experimentation
     - ☐ Delegates authority and responsibility
     - ☐ Inspires a shared vision by enlisting values, hopes, and dreams
     - ☐ Fosters a learning environment
     - ☐ Promotes shared information and collaborative problem solving
     - ☐ Models behavior—"walks the talk"
     - ☐ Appreciates diversity of style and behavior
     - ☐ Focuses on developing people
     - ☐ Gives "carefrontive," not confrontive, feedback and helps people learn and grow
     - ☐ Encourages self-expression and open discussion of conflict

   - **Employee**
     - ☐ Takes responsibility for actions
     - ☐ Speaks out about problems and ways to work better
     - ☐ Seeks to solve problems, not to place blame
     - ☐ Sees network of "customer" relationships, internal and external
     - ☐ Is willing to engage in inquiry about assumptions

(continued next page)

Changes to Create Empowerment (Continued)

2. Relationships

- ☐ Commitment to collaboration
- ☐ Mutual trust and respect
- ☐ Engagement of others in decisions
- ☐ Shared accountability, rewards, and penalties
- ☐ Helpfulness to each other
- ☐ Communication of all relevant information
- ☐ Cross-departmental learning
- ☐ Focus on process and learning

3. Organizational Structure

- ☐ Reward systems—Rewards are consistent with organizational values.
- ☐ Shared values—Commonly accepted values are well articulated and widely understood.
- ☐ Human-capital focus—Individual high performance (physical, emotional, and spiritual) is developed and maintained.
- ☐ Work autonomy and job flexibility—The organization is responsive to individual life-cycle demands, provides lateral and vertical expansion of skills and contributions, and is committed to mastery of multiple skills.
- ☐ Commitment to high quality and customer service—The organization pays attention to the marketplace, is flexible in its response, and keeps up a dialogue about needs.
- ☐ Commitment to communication—Information about vision, strategy, and direction is shared within the organization, and employee input is elicited and responded to.
- ☐ Creation of a community—People feel good about working together.
- ☐ Effective stress management and career development—People are allowed to practice self-care to avoid burnout and are supported to find resources to grow at work.

CHAPTER

5

Motivating Through Self-Esteem

MOTIVATING THROUGH SELF-ESTEEM

Where did the gung ho go? The dominant mood in a lot of American companies is one of fear and anxiety. Loyal corporate soldiers used to believe their employers would reward good work with job security, full benefits, and decent pay. Now they have serious doubts about whether they can expect anything beyond the next paycheck.

—Labor Day, Time Magazine

EMPOWERMENT TIP

Motivate people by VIP: Validation, Information, and Participation.

Empowerment Is Total

People at work want to make a difference. A recent Gallup Poll noted that nearly three-quarters of workers want more meaning from their work. Yet most theories of work motivation assume the opposite: people basically don't care, and that they need to be watched carefully to make sure they work. The empowered manager motivates people by getting them involved and committed to the tasks that need to be done, not by forcing them. He or she uses the natural desire of people to be helpful and make a difference and molds it into focused activity. Too often, organizations only reward people for individual effort, not for teamwork. The empowered manager tries to build new rewards for teamwork, sharing, and helping each other.

These employees need to be empowered!

Work Satisfies Human Needs

It used to be that U.S. companies had forgotten their customers. Today it seems that they have forgotten their employees.

—Japanese executive, *AMA report*

The view that the organization and the individual are in conflict is questioned by the concept of empowerment. Empowerment suggests that the organization can satisfy the individual and also get what it needs. It can be a win-win, mutually beneficial, relationship.

It is amazing that organizations with powerful, 21st-century technical systems put them to use in organizations molded on early 20th-century bureaucratic principles. And they motivate people using 19th-century assumptions about human nature!

Many managers spend much of their time disqualifying people, making up reasons why their people won't do what the organization wants them to.

Managers say to themselves:

"They aren't motivated."

"People don't care."

"They aren't able."

"They're not reliable."

"They just won't do it."

They expect the worst from people. In truth, this is what happens when people are motivated by old-style management. Not surprisingly, the manager usually finds that these negative beliefs turn out to be correct. He or she is right, but for the wrong reasons. The manager doesn't see that he or she has created a self-fulfilling prophesy. By acting in such a way that the team did not achieve the desired results, the manager proved his or her negative assumptions to be correct. The key to motivating people is to look at your own attitudes and assumptions about what they want and about how to create a positive work environment.

What Motivates Your Employees?

Do you know what your employees really want? Their answers could surprise you. A survey of 2,000 workers and their immediate supervisors found that what managers think employees want and what employees really want are at opposite ends of the spectrum.

Rank the following most common motivators in terms of how effective they would be for motivating you and your employees:

Motivator	Ranking for You	Ranking for Your Employees
Money		
Job security		
Promotion		
Personal development		
Working conditions		
Interesting work		
Loyalty from the company		
Tactful disciplining		
Appreciation		
Flexibility about personal needs		
Feeling informed		

In responding to the survey, managers consistently saw themselves as being motivated by different factors than their employees. They felt that the best ways to motivate employees were the traditional trio of motivators: job security, financial rewards, and job advancement.

The problem is that the traditional motivators are scarce resources for a company. They simply cannot be provided under today's working conditions. So the majority of employees would remain unsatisfied if these were the supervisor's primary means of motivation.

Everyone Can Be a VIP

There is some good news, however. The survey also asked all the employees in the company to say what really motivated them. They picked a very different set of motivators as most effective. In fact, the traditional trio of motivators were the bottom three of their list. The primary motivators of the empowered workplace are what we call the VIP motivators:

Validation
- Respect for employees as people
- Flexibility to meet personal needs
- Encouragement of learning, growth, and new skills

Information
- Knowing why things are being done
- Getting inside information about the company

Participation
- Employees having control over how they do their work
- Involvement in decisions that affect them

Looking at the above list, are they scarce resources for a work group? No—in fact they can be freely available to everyone. Every manager can provide respect, information, and participation in a workplace.

The key to creating an empowered workplace is to tap into these new motivators, to create a workplace where people want to work. That means realizing that your employees will be more likely to help you get a job done if they feel they are treated like grown-up people, if they feel the organization will consider their needs, if they know why they are doing things, and if they get to help decide the best way to get the job done.

Looking at your work group, list several activities that will help you add VIP to your workplace. Ask your team members for their suggestions to add to your list!

Validation:

_____

Information:

_____

Participation:

_____

How Anger Affects Work

One's attitude toward oneself is the single most important factor in healing and staying well.
—Bernie Siegel, *Love, Medicine and Miracles*

The pressure of today's workplace is immense. When a manager feels under pressure, he or she often tends to react with behavior that is less than helpful. This occurs when, for example, the manager feels frustrated or has difficulty in knowing how they can get the job done.

Then the manager faces his team and responds to his feelings with anger, blame, heightened control, and limited information. Criticism and control interfere with employees wanting to make their workplace more empowered. Management by fear has its adherents, but over time it tends to backfire.

CRITICISM

How do you respond to criticism? Does it motivate you? Most people say no, but managers persist in blaming and criticizing employees. Try to notice how often you criticize others. Think of some other ways that you could offer suggestions or point out difficulties without criticizing the other person.

The tendency to criticize others has several consequences.
- People avoid a person whom they expect will criticize them.
- People withhold information.
- People get angry.
- People feel more stress.
- People make more mistakes.
- People become more cautious and withhold creative ideas.
- People avoid bringing bad news.

> **EMPOWERMENT TIP**
> Try saying three positive things to employees before you offer a critical message.

KEEPING CONTROL AND ALWAYS BEING RIGHT

We all know managers who want to be in control of everything and who will never even consider that they might have made a mistake. Such a management style, no matter how talented the manager, has one effect on subordinates. It makes them care less, contribute less, and think only in terms of pleasing the boss, not getting the job done.

Many workplaces are diminished because employees spend all their time trying to figure out what the manager wants, never really exploring what doing a good job would look like. The other effect of this behavior is that employees don't take initiative. They try to clear everything with the manager. Things slow way down when everything needs to be checked upstairs.

Self-Esteem at the Workplace

People spend one-third of their waking lives at work, and the manager must remember that the workplace is probably the most important community a person lives in. Empowerment is the building and enhancement of basic self-esteem in the workplace. People who are allowed to feel good about themselves can give more to their work. They are also physically healthier. The outcome is healthy people in healthy places.

In situations where people are not free to work at the maximum effectiveness and their self-esteem is constantly under attack, stress claims, illness, and absenteeism go up. Morale goes down. Productivity plummets. We can look at health, productivity, and satisfaction with work as three interlocking circles:

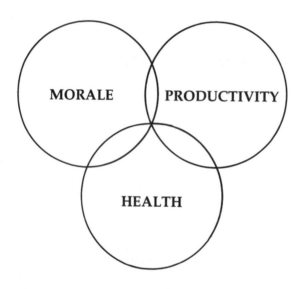

Workers need to be encouraged to find their satisfaction in how well they do their jobs. The key to motivation in an empowered environment is to understand that what gives people the most personal satisfaction is doing a good job. When people are given information, skills, tools, and responsibility, they thrive. Self-esteem is enhanced when people are allowed to exercise more judgment in their work. In the traditional pyramid structure, only a few people are allowed to win. The goal of the circle is for everyone to win.

Self-esteem is nurtured by achieving goals. The successful organization needs to create a structure and a climate in which people may be successful. Unfortunately, most performance reviews are conducted by people who don't feel good about themselves—this is one of the prime ways in which organizations tear people up.

The New Work Contract: Mutuality

Hereinafter, the employee will assume full responsibility for his own career—for keeping his qualifications up to date, for getting himself moved to the next position at the right time, for salting away funds for retirement, and, most daunting of all, for achieving job satisfaction. The company, while making no promises, will endeavor to provide a conducive environment, economic exigencies permitting.

—Walter Kiechel, *Fortune*

Employees in all companies bemoan the loss of what they call job security, the sense that the company will take care of them if they do their job. In some companies the sense of betrayal is deep and destructive when the company begins to shift toward an empowered culture. People feel that the company no longer cares and that the rules are changing. Initially, they feel angry and fearful.

But the rules have not been changed by the companies. They have been changed by the new work environment, which forces companies to work harder and be more accountable for themselves. Every company has to learn to do more with less, and in a continually changing environment no company can offer real security.

So how can you keep your employees from withdrawing into negativity and passivity when the company attempts to have them take more responsibility? That is every manager's motivation dilemma. The answer lies in creating real understanding that the rules of relationship between the company and its employees have changed fundamentally.

Forging the New Work Contract

Every company has an implicit psychological contract or agreement—it agrees to give something to employees in return for their commitment to the company. This agreement traditionally involved elements of paternalism or dependency, in which employees gave up some of their initiative and freedom in return for feeling taken care of by the company and its managers.

Today, the company can't have this minimal level of commitment from employees. It needs people who are willing to put more of their intelligence, creativity, and energy to making the company work. The employee has to be willing to change jobs, to learn new skills, to get the jobs done that the company needs.

Today, the new employee-employer agreement is one of mutuality, where two parties agree to work together to achieve a result. The company can't take care of its employees unlimitedly, but it can guarantee them rewards for what they give. It is a contract for here-and-now involvement, not for the future. It is conditional and based on performance.

BENEFITS OF MUTUALITY

Why should your employees agree to this more limited protection, let alone feel good about it? The answer has to do with self-reliance. There are two benefits. But it takes time before they become apparent and you experience them.

First, the employee is asked to be more creatively and actively involved in the work of the company. This new workstyle is more satisfying and more motivating. A person can learn and grow and see the results of his input.

Second, as a person takes responsibility for her future, the feeling of dependency on the company grows less. As people learn more skills and see that these skills are useful, they can work with the inner confidence that, even if the company can't take care of them, they can take care of themselves. This gives them a deeper sense of self-esteem and self-confidence for taking care of their future. Even if they have to leave a company, they feel they have learned useful skills and been rewarded adequately, and they can find work elsewhere. They can feel that the time was worthwhile.

Foundations for Mutuality

The traditional manager is responsible for monitoring the performance of employees. That role shifts in an empowered organization. The manager is not responsible for performance, but rather for creating an environment where people can perform. Like a coach, the manager supports and guides employees to increasing levels of performance.

Keys to Negotiating a Mutual Contract

- **Shared assessment**
- **Problem-solving orientation**
- **Growth and learning**

---

1. Shared Assessment

The primary goal of a performance assessment is to help the individual do better, not to punish or reward. Why is the manager the only one who evaluates performance? Frequently, the manager has less information about who is doing what than other team members or other coworkers.

In an empowered organization where responsibility is shared, so is the responsibility for evaluation. This means that both parties to an assessment conduct an evaluation. The employee begins by assessing his or her own performance according to preset goals. In addition, input is often sought from several team members and other coworkers. The person being assessed might select four or five people to be evaluators. The goal is to open up the process, so that the most relevant people give feedback to each other.

In your team or company, who does the evaluation now?

_____

_____

How might you involve more people?

_____

_____

Foundations for Mutuality (Continued)

2. Problem-Solving Orientation

The traditional manager was a person who always knew what to do and could tell you. In today's organization, problems are so new and complex that nobody is certain how to get things done. When problems arise or the unexpected occurs, the role of the manager is to help others solve them. He is not responsible for finding solutions. Rather, he should work with the person to go back and discover possibilities, to see what options are available. The goal is to help the employee with a problem learn how to solve it.

It is often difficult for a manager, especially a person trained to think that being decisive is what management is all about, to adopt this problem-solving orientation. Yet the manager who challenges people to find solutions will find that her people develop their individual ability to solve problems.

What would it take for you to develop a more problem-solving focus?

_____

_____

3. Growth and Learning

In the new organization, employees want to learn, grow, and develop their abilities. This means they need to have a continual series of new challenges, and they need to rotate or move between routine and repetitious jobs. Although an organization has many routine jobs, empowered organizations are finding several mechanisms that offer employees the chance to learn and grow:

- **Cross-training**, to expand their ability and help people understand each other's jobs.

- **Job rotation** into other areas of the company, to develop skills and perspective.

- **Participation** in task forces and other ad hoc problem-solving groups, to help improve the company, develop quality, and define new products and services.

- **Delegating and job enrichment**, to offer employees more responsibility in their work by delegating tasks to them and expanding their roles.

CHAPTER

6

Developing Collaborative Relationships

DEVELOPING COLLABORATIVE RELATIONSHIPS

When you're going to address a problem, get the people who have something to contribute in the way of creativity if not direct responsibility. Get them together. Turn them loose.

—CEO John Smale, *Harvard Business Review*

EMPOWERMENT TIP

The manager must learn to shift from a directive to a collaborative style of action. People in a group need to learn to solve problems together and to share authority, control, responsibility, and rewards.

The Death of Paternalism

In pyramid organizations, the manager's job was to take care of things, like a parent. This often left the employees feeling like children. They expected the manager and the organization to meet their needs. And the manager felt the burden of being solely responsible for the team's results. This ''father/mother knows best'' tradition leaves the manager burdened and the employee powerless.

As change happens more quickly and the skills demanded by the workplace change, it will take both managers and employees working together to be the co-creators of success. Instead of one person working alone to solve problems, the new manager in the empowered organization must see his or her team as collaborators in getting the job done. Empowerment means seeing the team in a different way and behaving differently.

History of Collaboration

You may be asking, ''Isn't this what participative management was all about? Is this just the same old stuff with a different name?'' Many waves of management theory have included seemingly collaborative approaches. Here is a brief history.

- In the 1950s managers learned to be friendly.

- In the 1960s managers became sensitive to needs and motivation.

- In the 1970s managers asked employees for help.

- In the 1980s managers initiated a lot of meetings.

- In the 1990s managers share ownership of tasks and rewards for results.

The difference now is that it's not just the manager doing the participating, making it happen. Now with collaboration, the employee has a 50% responsibility to make it work.

UNDERSTANDING COLLABORATION

Collaboration is when a group of people share the planning, implementing, and fruits of activity. It is a full partnership. This doesn't necessarily mean that nobody is the leader. It is just that leadership is different.

The nature of real team collaboration is often confused with communication and participation. Several steps represent moves in the direction of real collaboration.

STEPS TO COLLABORATION

Step 1: Paternalism—taking care of people without telling them.

Step 2: Communication—telling people why things are done and keeping them informed.

Step 3: Participation—asking people for ideas and input.

Step 4: Collaboration—sharing planning, implementation, accountability, and rewards.

Learning to Solve Problems Together

Does somebody really always have to be in charge? Conventional wisdom says that one person has to be the leader, to make decisions. The empowered organization questions that wisdom by suggesting that people can work and make decisions together.

While the new workplace may have a leader, the role of the leader is very different. The leader is reponsible for setting up a high-performance environment—for managing the context, rather than producing the results.

> *The new leader is responsible for the process, not the outcomes.*

But that's not the way we were raised and it's not a style of operation that many of us have seen much before. It will take time, patience, false starts, and a lot of practice.

PITFALLS OF PASSIVITY

People become passive if they don't expect to be asked to contribute. They stop listening to themselves and turn themselves off. They don't listen to their new ideas and don't look for ways to improve their work and the organization.

Employees who have never been asked to be in charge before will be skeptical and distrustful. "Why should I care?" they will say. "What will I get in return?" Since employees are being asked to shoulder more responsibility for results, they must in turn receive more from the organization in rewards.

That's not all they need. They also need to learn the new ways of empowerment, to develop the new skills for working together and sharing decisions and reponsibility. You can't learn this overnight, and you can't learn it without training, practice, and continual support and reinforcement.

This chapter will help you, as a manager, begin to define the new collaborative role. You need to learn to give up control by letting go. It's hard to learn at first, but the rewards are immense.

The Experience of Collaboration

Most people do have experiences of collaboration in their lives, even if they don't have it at work. All of us have been involved in collaborative experiences, where everyone was in charge or leadership was shared. Think back to your own work experience as well as outside activities like the PTA, community or church groups, sports, and other activities.

What were the hallmarks of these activities?

_____

_____

What got you motivated?

_____

_____

How did each person in the group get to exercise leadership?

_____

_____

What are the activities or approaches that increase people's willingness and ability to collaborate?

_____

_____

What do people do that make you feel less collaborative?

_____

_____

What are the key elements that make up a collaborative environment?

_____

_____

Directive and Collaborative Styles

Most people experience themselves as combining the directive and the collaborative style. You may find yourself switching styles between home and work. In the traditional organization the directive style was more usual. In the network organization the collaborative style is preferred.

Both styles are important. Some tasks are best accomplished with one or another. The goal is to have fluency in both styles. Take a moment to review the following list, which contrasts the two styles.

Directive	Collaborative
You alone are responsible.	Shared responsibility.
High-intensity persuasion.	Low-key encouragement.
Prescribes what to do.	Facilitates group discovery.
You assume you know the way.	You ask others to help.
Minimal feedback.	Communication and controversy.
Midcourse correction is difficult.	Flexible, easy to shift direction.
Used when there is little prior commitment.	Used when everyone shares goal.
No time for pilot tests or questions.	Makes use of pilot projects and continual evaluation of results.
Top-down communication.	Two-way communication.

Comparing Management Styles

You might want to compare these two management styles from the above lists and from your own experience. Certain times and situations demand directive management, and other situations demand a more collaborative style. Today's complex work demands more collaborative management to solve its problems.

Directive Management:

What are its benefits?

How do you feel when you use this leadership style?

What are the drawbacks of this style?

Collaborative Management:

What are its benefits?

How do you feel when you use this leadership style?

What are the drawbacks of this style?

Concerns and Fears about Collaboration

If the only style you've seen is the directive style, it may not be easy to experiment with the collaborative style. In fact, it may be very unsettling. You may feel you are being asked to be weak, indecisive, or ineffective. Sometimes a manager thinks that collaboration is losing control.

What do you say to yourself when you think about increasing employees' involvement in decision making?

What evidence or experience do you have for this being true?

In the end, you need to test your concerns with action. You need to take the risk and let people collaborate. It may feel unsettling the first few times, but you can expect to be surprised by the results.

Checking Your Style

Which style of action is most like you? Think of the issues you face as a manager. For each of the situations below, circle the number that most closely approximates how you feel or respond to each situation. Circle 1 if the statement on the left of the page is always true and the statement on the right never. Circle 7 if the statement on the right of the page is always true. Circle 4 if both statements are equally true. If one statement is more often true, but not always, circle a number in between.

1. When I have a problem...

I try to solve it myself   I get help from others

    1   2   3   4   5   6   7

2. If somebody is doing something and I think I know a better way...

I tell them to do it differently   I suggest other ways

    1   2   3   4   5   6   7

3. Before making a decision...

I consider it carefully   I seek input from others

    1   2   3   4   5   6   7

4. When people make mistakes...

I come down hard on them   I help them learn what went wrong

    1   2   3   4   5   6   7

5. The most important motivator for my group is...

Pleasing me   Doing the job well

    1   2   3   4   5   6   7

6. When I learn new information that affects the group...

I make the necessary adjustments   I share it as soon as possible

    1   2   3   4   5   6   7

Checking Your Style (Continued)

7. The group works best when I...

Tell people what to do   Help people work together

    1   2   3   4   5   6   7

8. When I'm not around...

                                  I feel confident the team is

I worry about things getting done   doing what need to be done

    1   2   3   4   5   6   7

9. When it comes down to the wire...

                                  Everyone feels responsible

I am responsible for our results   for our results

    1   2   3   4   5   6   7

10. When there are assignments and schedules to be done...

It's easiest for me to do them   I have people do them together

    1   2   3   4   5   6   7

11. When reporting to outside groups and top management...

                                  I share reporting with

I do the reporting   other team members

    1   2   3   4   5   6   7

12. When there is bad news or a problem...

                                  My team members let me

I have to discover it myself   know quickly

    1   2   3   4   5   6   7

Understanding Your Scores

Add up all your scores on all items.

- Scores below 24 indicate a directive style.
- Scores above 60 indicate a collaborative style.
- Scores between 25 and 60 indicate a mixed or flexible style.

C H A P T E R

7

Establishing Facilitative Leadership

MAKE INDIVIDUALITY WORK FOR YOU

ESTABLISHING FACILITATIVE LEADERSHIP

Learning is the new form of labor. It's no longer a separate activity that occurs either before one enters the workplace or in remote classroom settings.... Learning is the heart of productive activity.

—Shoshana Zuboff, *The Age of the Smart Machine*

EMPOWERMENT TIP

The new leader must learn to step back and create an environment to allow each individual to learn, grow, develop, contribute, and excel.

The Facilitative Leader and the Empowered Team

The basic building unit of the empowered organization is not the individual achiever, but the coordinated group of people—the team. These are not simply a group of individuals who report to the same person. Like an athletic team, they form a coordinated unit where everyone knows their part but is free to shine and achieve.

The leader of the team is not the person who gives the order to march. The leader is the person who is in charge of the personal development of the team members— the person who creates the environment for performance, learning, and development. This new type of leader is called the facilitative leader.

For a facilitative leader, developing a climate for team performance is an essential skill for creating empowerment. In the currents of change in organizations, one of the most frequent is the flattening of the organization. Pyramids are letting the air out, and in the process layers of middle managers change their roles.

Middle managers must do more than oversee. They must help people learn, grow, and develop. They need to help the team work together, not just check up on the work of a bunch of individuals. Middle managers are an endangered species, unless they adapt to the new workplace!

The facilitative leader is a teacher, a cheerleader, a coach. The new leader/manager is also a communication link, connecting the team to other groups and integrating their efforts with those of others. In fact, in a circle organization, a person is usually part of several teams, not just of one.

Creating a Climate for Learning

The facilitative leader helps the team develop a learning environment. We understand individual learning, but what does it mean for a team or organization to learn? It means that the team not only gets a job done, but does it in such a way that they learn how to do it again, even do it again more effecively. The key skill is not simply getting the job done, but also learning how to learn. The team continually faces new challenges and new dilemmas.

Learning is an attitude of openness to new ideas, a willingness to explore new possibilities, and the discipline to test them effectively. A learning team must allow creativity and value the exploration of new territory. Everyone must know how to learn.

ARE YOU A LEARNER?

In order to help others become learners, you need to look at your own openness to learning. If you as a manager fear or avoid your own learning, you will hold your team back from growing. Use the checklist below to see if you yourself are open to learning. Check ☑ the statements that are true for you. For each one you check, try to write down a concrete example of your behavior in that regard.

- ☐ **1.** I want to learn new things.
  For example, _____
- ☐ **2.** I am curious about how other people do their jobs.
  For example, _____
- ☐ **3.** I learn about other groups and companies doing similar work.
  For example, _____
- ☐ **4.** I can handle the frustration of changing in mid course.
  For example, _____
- ☐ **5.** I question whether the way I do things is the best way.
  For example, _____
- ☐ **6.** I try to look for aspects of a problem I have not considered.
  For example, _____
- ☐ **7.** I listen to other people's ideas before I suggest my way.
  For example, _____
- ☐ **8.** I know how to ask for help when I don't know something.
  For example, _____
- ☐ **9.** There is always another way to get a job done.
  For example, _____
- ☐ **10.** I try to expand my skills in different directions every year.
  For example, _____

_____ TOTAL (A facilitative leader should score 7 or above.)

Blame Placing versus Problem Solving

When a group or even a pair of people encounters a problem, the first instinct is to find out who is to blame. Somebody or something is blamed, and everyone feels less uncomfortable—except, of course, the person blamed. But what does blame accomplish? Not very much.

The empowering group has abolished blame as an activity. When there is a problem, the people involved talk about how to solve it, not who is to blame. The group asks what systems broke down and assumes that the difficulty more often than not had several causes. The group looks for ways to do things better, not ways to point the finger. This creates a learning atmosphere where everybody looks for ways to correct mistakes, and nobody feels ashamed or singled out.

SEARCHING FOR PROBLEMS

Many business crises arise because the organization was not willing to look at early signs of difficulty. The empowered team must continually search for problems, not wait to be hit with them. Therefore, it must trust individuals with hunches, must seek out problem areas aggressively, and must be open to seeing unexpected effects of their work. They may not have all the data at first—and they may be wrong. They must communicate with the organizational groups who are their suppliers and customers.

It is very difficult for an individual, and for a team, to stop trying to protect themselves, becoming defensive, and avoiding looking directly at difficulties. Nobody likes to hear bad news or be confronted with potential crises. But an empowered team needs to learn the skills to face problems as they arise.

LIBERATING CREATIVITY

The learning team must seek new ideas and new possibilities. Whenever they reach a choice point or need a decision, they must strive not to do the first thing they think of or fall back on the usual response. They must learn to step back and try to discover new ways. Since people are naturally attached to their old ways and form habits that are very hard to break, openness to learning is worth cultivating. But a willingness to entertain alternatives is a difficult attitude to sustain.

The Facilitative Leader Role

Building a team that is open to learning is the most difficult task of the empowered leader. Here are some of the key qualities of this new leader.

- **Leads with vision, not tradition**

  He aligns people with a vision of what they want to become. The vision is generated by everyone and is inspiring and meaningful.

- **Learner, not teacher**

  She knows what she doesn't know and is willing to learn. She is not committed to the old ways as the only wisdom.

- **Focus on process, not content**

  He seeks to get the process going instead of trying to determine the content of how the group works.

- **Enabler, not controller**

  She doesn't try to keep control. She delegates and sets people free to perform. She shares responsibility and the authority to act.

- **Coach, not expert**

  He helps people learn and develop skills. He always expects more of people.

- **Linkers, not hoarders**

  She shares information across groups and links joint projects. She spends time seeking information and linking the team's work with that of other groups.

- **Emotional literacy, not technical skill**

  He understands that change is difficult and that people have difficult feelings. He is sensitive to the needs of the staff, finding ways to create mutuality. He encourages resistant and stuck team members to grow.

Shifting to Facilitative Leadership

To accomplish this shift to facilitative leadership, managers and employees need a number of elements to succeed.

	Managers Need	Employees Need
Support	structure, incentives	feedback, encouragement
Resources	models, coaching	tools, practice
Direction	vision, inspiration	goals, measurements
Knowledge	training, examples	training, role models

Look at each of these elements and write what you are doing to provide these important elements for change for yourself and your team.

	Managers Need	Employees Need
Support		
Resources		
Direction		
Knowledge		

8

Building Empowered Teams

BUILDING EMPOWERED TEAMS

> **EMPOWERMENT TIP**
>
> An empowered team is one that sees itself as one unit, that is clear about where it is going, and that shares the central qualities of work, power, skills, control, authority, and rewards.

The Nature of the Empowered Team

The team is where empowerment grows. The most important ingredient of empowerment is the direct relationship between you and the people you work with. The newest research points directly to this work unit as the focus of change. People tend to change in relationship, not from information. So the focus of empowerment is the relationships you build at work.

Techniques to Create Empowerment

Managers have tried many things to try to get more empowerment into their teams. Check ☑ the ones that you have tried.

- ☐ Suggestion systems

- ☐ Employee of the month

- ☐ Training

- ☐ Team building

- ☐ Quality circles

- ☐ Motivational talks

- ☐ Job enrichment

Most of these things were not the magic potion. That's because the manager was setting the structure—it wasn't a collaborative process. Collaborative decision making requires skill and training. Individual mindsets and organizational structure also play a part. There is no magic menu. None of these techniques does it by itself.

Empowerment Focus

The most important ingredient of empowerment is the direct relationship between you and the people you work with.

The next most important effect on employee empowerment comes from peers, team members, suppliers, and other people in the work environment.

Another important influence is upper management—their leadership, direction, and vision.

Finally, there are the organizational systems, structures, and policies.

Group Synergy

An empowered team uses all the talent of the players to create an even better result. This synergy of many people working together often produces exciting results.

For this synergy to develop there is a foundation of elements that leads to empowered teamwork.

Things that need to be shared in an empowered team:

- Ownership
- Responsibility
- Authority
- Power
- Rewards
- Energy

Often there are job-related ingredients that keep empowerment from growing in a team. How many of these are present in your group? Check ☑ those that apply to your group.

- ☐ Jobs with no meaning
- ☐ Little feedback (success or correction)
- ☐ Fighting fires rather than solving problems
- ☐ No flexibility
- ☐ No time to see the bigger picture
- ☐ Confusion
- ☐ Lack of dialogue (listening and solving)

74

Sharing Responsibility

Many times managers view empowerment as a form of abandoning responsibility. Let's be very clear:

> *Sharing responsibility does not mean abandoning responsibility.*

When a manager delegates responsibility, he or she has three choices: keep the work, delegate without decision-making authority, or delegate authority.

The manager has the choice of which option to pursue. Making one of these choices is taking situational control.

EXPANDING RESPONSIBILITY

As the manager becomes more empowering, there is added responsibility for setting the direction of the group, for coaching, and for more accurate performance feedback.

The empowered manager has responsibility for setting the process for:

- Creating mission and vision
- Offering guidance, support, and coaching
- Assessing performance as it happens

What have you done in each of these areas?

Creating mission and vision: _____

_____

Offering guidance: _____

_____

Assessing performance: _____

_____

Action Ideas for Team Empowerment

1. Present a challenge and have the team self-nominate a group to work together to solve the problem. Set a time for the group to produce a result, but do not interfere. When they come back with the solution, engage in a learning dialogue to select an option.

2. Establish a clear mission together. Set aside some time to talk about the reason your team exists. Encourage everyone to give ideas. Write down one or two sentences that describes your group's purpose.

3. Teach people the skills for problem solving and brainstorming. Choose one team member to facilitate with these techniques. Don't interrupt or take back control.

4. Provide time and place for meetings. Train your group in meeting facilitation. Take turns in running your meetings with these techniques. Learn from each other.

5. Give clear feedback about performance. Establish some guidelines for how to give feedback: no attacks, criticism, or nonchangeable elements. As a team, pick one area of performance—such as communication flow or problem solving—and have everyone give feedback to everyone about that area.

6. Focus on the positive, and celebrate the reward success.

EXAMPLES OF EMPOWERED TEAM RESPONSIBILITIES

Many times managers think that they will just wave the magic wand and the team will become empowered overnight. This is a common mistake, leading to disappointment and frustration. The empowerment process is a series of learning steps. The following are some places to start the empowerment process.

- Schedule vacations.
- Select a leader for a specific project.
- Divide work.
- Monitor performance on criteria that the team sets up.
- Examine how work gets done.

Levels of Decision Making

Decision making is the core process of working with your team. It is important to understand that there are different levels of participation in decision making. The lowest level of participation is telling people what you will do. One of the highest levels is where everybody makes decisions together. You can even go one step further and delegate a decision to the team, taking yourself out of the decision-making structure altogether.

The following decision scale represents the levels of decision making that a manager can use in building team performance.

Decision Scale

Level Five: Delegate
You ask them to decide.
They take control.

Level Four: Collaboration
Reach a decision that everyone likes.
Everyone takes full responsibility.

Level Three: Dialogue
Discuss each issue thoroughly before you decide.
Everybody goes along with the decision.

Level Two: Input
Ask for input before making a decision.
Listen to comments.

Level One: Directive
Tell them what you have decided.
Ask what they think about it.

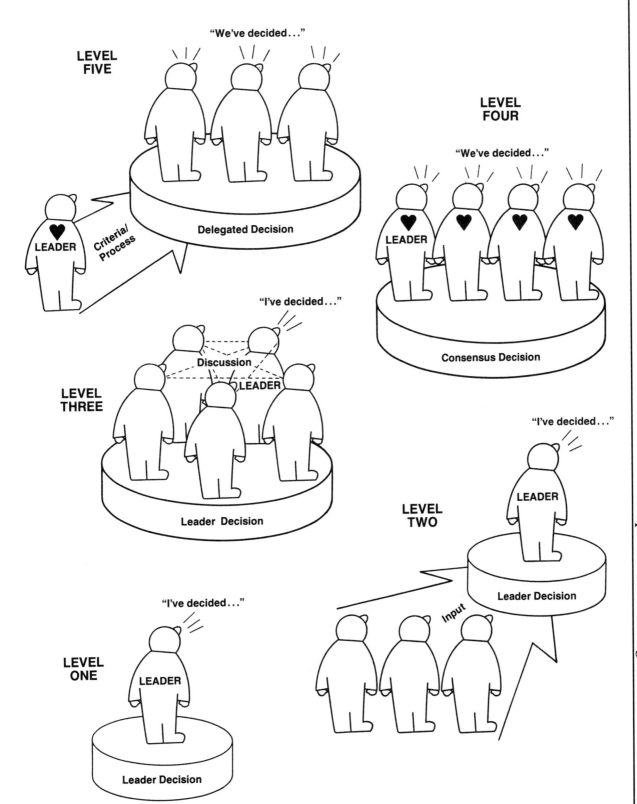

Thinking About Your Decision Style

How do you make decisions? Do you use the same way over and over, or do you vary it according to the situation or the person involved? Think about recent decisions you have made.

What process did you use to make them?

_____

_____

_____

_____

At what point did you consult others?

_____

_____

_____

_____

Sometimes you want to let people know about a difficulty as soon as you hear about it. Other times, you make a decision or check out possibilities before letting others know.

GENERATING COMMITMENT

The more you consult with your team, the more time it will take. However, there is a trade-off: the more people are involved in making a decision the more committed they will be to implementing it. It takes more time to get more commitment.

Also, when a team works together to make a decision it takes more possibilities into account and makes better decisions. Although they take longer, participatory decisions are usually more creative. They consider more information, and they are more flexible—everyone feels knowledgeable enough to handle unexpected consequences and unpredicted difficulties without feeling confused.

Clarifying Team Decisions

Think of decisions that are being made in your team. Identify at what level each decision is being made, and why. What would it take to bring it up to a higher level?

Decision	What level?	Why?	What would it take to move up?
1. _____	____	_____	_____
		_____	_____
2. _____	____	_____	_____
		_____	_____
3. _____	____	_____	_____
		_____	_____
4. _____	____	_____	_____
		_____	_____
5. _____	____	_____	_____
		_____	_____

Decision Funnel

Empowered decision making can happen at all levels. There are times when level 1 is very appropriate. What is important is how you do it—with explanation and consideration, or as an edict handed down. The level the decision is made at should be clear to the team.

Team members have responsibility at each level of this process. The diagram below shows some of the team members' input at each level.

Manager/Leader	Level	Team Member
Lay out process and criteria by which decisions are to be reached. Embrace the decisions.	1	Accept responsibility for decision-making process.
Participation and acknowledgement of consensual process.	2	Work on outcome till it feels right. Embrace the decision
Listen and discuss participant's input. Make decision.	3	Active participation, voice opinions. Support decision.
Listen to input. Make clear decisions.	4	Voice opinions on time.
Give a direct command.	5	Listen carefully.

↑ Time Needed

↑ Commitment To Decision

Double-Responsibility Decision Making

Decision-making levels have responsibilities on each side—for the manager and for the employee. The process of empowerment elicits the expectations that each member has in the process.

Think of decision making in your group. At what level of responsibility and involvement are your team members participating?

_____

What could you do to encourage their participation at the next higher level?

_____

_____

_____

_____

_____

Elements of an Empowered Team

The job of today's manager is to build an empowered team. To do this, some important elements need to be developed. Managers and employees share in the development of these elements. They are the foundation of the empowered decision-making process:

- Respect
- Control
- Responsibility
- Information
- Decision-making
- Skills

RESPECT

There is respect when people expect the best from each other, and when they assume that others have constructive motivations. Each person has personal needs, agendas, and preferences that must be negotiated. The organization can't always come first.

What are some of the ways you can create mutual respect with your team members?

_____

_____

INFORMATION

People who work together need complete information. The manager needs to inform people clearly and completely and then let them make conclusions. Information should flow freely not be hoarded or hidden from certain people or certain levels of employees.

What are some of the ways you can inform your team more fully?

_____

_____

CONTROL AND DECISION MAKING

People want to make decisions about how they reach goals and the best way to get a job done. Empowering managers don't assume they know but ask people to work with them to decide how to do things. This may take longer at the start, but it builds complete agreement and higher commitment to getting the best results.

What are some of the ways you can share power with your team?

_____

_____

RESPONSIBILITY

Empowerment means that responsibility is not all on the manager's shoulders. He or she can count on help and will share the rewards and credit with everyone. When this happens, the manager sleeps better and feels less helpless and deserted when there is a crisis.

What are some of the ways you can share responsibility with your team?

_____

_____

SKILLS

People need new skills, and they need to keep learning to keep up with the organization's needs. People need to have the opportunity to learn, so they can be true partners.

What are some of the ways you can facilitate your team's learning?

_____

_____

C H A P T E R

9

Influencing
Organizational Change

INFLUENCING ORGANIZATIONAL CHANGE

Leadership is liberating people to do what is required of them in the most effective and most human way possible. [Removes obstacles, enables followers to reach full potential.]

Leaders must be clear about their own beliefs—have thought through their assumptions about human nature—the role of the organization and how to measure performance.

Leadership is more tribal than scientific, more a weaving of relationships than amassing information.

—Max DePree, *Leadership Is an Art*

EMPOWERMENT TIP

Become an empowerment force in the whole organization. Support empowerment and challenge the organization to grow.

EMPOWERMENT AND THE ORGANIZATION

Empowerment is not just an individual or team effort. Organizational structure, policy, values, incentives, and culture must reinforce individual and team behavior. These structures are often the most challenging areas to change. Your power and influence as an individual manager is limited, and the act of questioning or challenging an organizational structure is risky.

In creating an empowered organization, a manager needs to be aware of how organizational policy contradicts the team behavior he or she is trying to reinforce. Where necessary, the manager must try to change the organizational policy. For example, it is difficult to get team members to work together and help each other when rewards and incentives are all for individual achievement. Why should people support each other?

Organizational Barriers

What are some of the areas where your organization's culture, structures, values, and ways of doing things conflict with the values of empowerment?

_____

_____

_____

The manager's role is to sponsor empowerment activities and to be an advocate for change within the organization. He or she needs to become a positive advocate for empowerment rather than feeling hemmed in and frustrated by the organization.

ORGANIZATIONAL ADVOCACY

Things that a manager has to do to influence upward thinking and protect empowerment on a team:

- **Challenge the organization**—ask questions, attend meetings, be a constructive advocate of empowerment.

- **Buffer the team**—make the changes you can at your team level. Work with your team to develop empowered relationships where you can.

- **Success by sharing results**—one of the outcomes of empowerment is increased team results. Measure them, celebrate them, and let other people know what you and your group did to make it happen.

- **Take risks**—try things that you would not normally do. Push yourself to your growing edge. Find encouragement with others who have gone there.

The development of organizational empowerment occurs at many levels. It involves the challenging of individual mindsets, the creation of new kinds of relationships, and the building of new organizational structures. The organizations that lead from the pyramid to the circle are creating a new form that will result in healthy people in healthy organizations. The development of these workplaces is an act of courage and persistence.

For More Information and Help

HeartWork Inc. offers consultation, presentations, and trainings that help leaders, managers, and employees develop the vision and skills necessary to make empowerment a reality in their organizations.

About the Authors

Dr. Dennis Jaffe is a founding partner of **HeartWork Inc.,** a San Francisco-based organizational development firm. He is a nationally recognized leader in the fields of managing organizational change, strategic management of human capital, visionary leadership, executive team development, and new models of health care. He consults to family businesses dealing with succession, communication, work-family issues and long-range planning, and with public organizations and corporations on managing organizational change, developing strategic visions, and designing collaborative workplaces.

Professional Background:
Dr. Jaffe earned his B.A. in philosophy, M.A. in management, and Ph.D. in sociology, all from Yale University. He is a professor at Saybrook Institute, where he serves as director of doctoral studies in Organizational Inquiry. He has been on the faculty at USC and UCLA. His professional training is in organizational development, and he is also a licensed clinical psychologist and family therapist.

Author:
Dr. Jaffe is the author of 12 books, including **Working With The Ones You Love;** the management best seller, **Take This Job and Love It; Managing Organizational Change; Self Renewal: Achieving High Performance in a High Stress Environment; Stress Map; Healing From Within** and **Empowerment**. Two of his books received the *Medical Self-Care Book Award.* He has published over 100 professional articles. His work has been featured in **The Wall Street Journal; Nation's Business; USA Today; Business Ethics; American Health; Psychology Today; San Francisco Business Times;** and **People**.

Designer of Tools for Business Excellence:
He is co-designer of corporate programs on **Managing the Human Side of Change**ˢᵐ, and has helped scores of organizations rebuild commitment and productivity after major change. His video, **Managing People Through Change**, was selected as one of the best of 1990 by **Human Resource Executive**. Dr. Jaffe co-designed the leading stress assessment tool, **Stressmap**ˢᵐ, used by over 2,000 organizations nationally, the new **Organizational Health Assessment**, and the **Family Business Assessment Inventory.**

About the Authors (Continued)

Dr. Cynthia Scott is a founding principal of **HeartWork Inc.,** a San Francisco-based organizational development firm. She is a recognized leader in the fields of strategic planning for human capital management, managing continual organizational change, and visionary leadership, Dr. Scott combines her formal education in Organizational Psychology, Anthropology and Health Planning and her insider's experience in corporate settings to bridge the gap between the traditional and organizational performance.

Professional Background:
Dr. Scott earned her B.A. in Anthropology, at the University of California, Berkeley, her M.P.H. in Health Planning and Administration, at the University of Michigan, and her Ph.D. in Clinical Psychology, from The Fielding Institute. She is currently a licensed clinical psychologist affiliated with the Department of Family and Community Medicine, University of California, San Francisco.

Author:
Dr. Scott is the author of 9 books: **Managing Organizational Change; Managing Personal Change; Self Renewal: Achieving High Performance in a High Stress Environment; Take This Job and Love It; StressMap;** and **Empowerment**. Her books for health professionals include: **Renewal Skills; Heal Thyself** and **Eldercare.**

Designer of Tools for Business Excellence:
She is the co-designer of the **Managing the Human Side of Change**ˢᵐ training programs, **The Empowerment Program**ˢᵐ**, StressMap**ˢᵐ, a stress assessment tool used by over 2,000 organizations and the **Organizational Health Assessment.** Her video, **Managing People Through Change,** was selected as one of the best of 1990 by **Human Resource Executive.**

For information about HeartWork consultation services call (415) 546-4488

Now that you have read *Empowerment,* please let us know how it has affected you and/or your organization.

Write to us at: HeartWork Inc.
461 Second Street, Suite 232
San Francisco, CA 94107-1416

NOTES

NOTES

NOTES

NOTES

OVER 150 BOOKS AND 35 VIDEOS AVAILABLE IN THE 50-MINUTE SERIES

We hope you enjoyed this book. If so, we have good news for you. This title is part of the best-selling *50-MINUTE*™ *Series* of books. All *Series* books are similar in size and identical in price. Many are supported with training videos.

To order *50-MINUTE* Books and Videos or request a free catalog, contact your local distributor or Crisp Publications, Inc., 1200 Hamilton Court, Menlo Park, CA 94025. Our toll-free number is (800) 442-7477.

50-Minute Series Books and Videos Subject Areas . . .

Management
Training
Human Resources
Customer Service and Sales Training
Communications
Small Business and Financial Planning
Creativity
Personal Development
Wellness
Adult Literacy and Learning
Career, Retirement and Life Planning

Other titles available from Crisp Publications in these categories

Crisp Computer Series
The Crisp Small Business & Entrepreneurship Series
Quick Read Series
Management
Personal Development
Retirement Planning